IDENTITY SWITCH

Becoming The Woman Who Gets What She Wants

April Mason

IDENTITY SWITCH

ISBN 978-0-9891254-6-8

Printed in the USA by

Contents

Foreword

I'm the type of man that gives credit where credit is due. When April shared the concept for her book with me, it excited me, and I knew I had to contribute. On my journey to becoming the Biggest Boss, I've had to undergo several identity switches myself. You can't make a bold statement that you will be rich forever without transforming yourself. Each stage of my journey required a different version of me.

I had to boss up, and I don't use that phrase lightly. It wasn't easy, but I had to do the hard work. I couldn't go to my next level being the old me. I will be joining the billionaires club soon, which will require me to undergo another identity switch, and Rozay is ready for the challenge.

I like what April represents. She is a walking example of the self-mastery that she teaches. She explains the steps to change your life so anyone can understand if they are ready. Please believe this is not a game; you must give one hundred percent.

April attended my Boss Up Conference. I watched how she handled business, how people responded to her, and how she worked the room. She exuded confidence and what she later taught me was femininity. It wasn't until she silenced the entire audience with her speech that I realized the incredible identity switch she had made herself. From our initial meeting, I would have never guessed she went through so much tragedy and hardships. Grab a glass of Belaire because you're about to learn what can be achieved when you make an identity shift.

The Boss, Rick Ross+

Introduction

It all started in 1999 when I experienced my first identity switch. I was unaware of the process I was about to embark on, but I knew something had to change. As a young mother, I had no clue what or who I was. I had three children to take care of, and it was no longer about me or my desires; the children came first.

I can recall being so frustrated with life. I felt my family did not set me up with the proper life tools to succeed. I placed blame and pointed the finger for a while, but I had to take responsibility for my own life. No matter what cards you are dealt, ultimately, you are responsible for the life you live. I had to let go of the anger because I accepted that my family did their best and gave me what was passed down to them.

During this time, I lived in a shelter in Richmond, CA. The residents there would often say, "You don't look like a shelter girl." I would always tell them I was simply passing through. Eventually, I moved to a transitional house across the street, where I had the vision. It was the vision of a woman in a business suit, a briefcase, beautiful flowing hair, confidence, a successful career, a plethora of high caliber men to choose from; she drove a convertible, had a beautifully furnished home, amazing girlfriends, an abundant bank account, and a life she was happy with. Very footloose and fancy-free.

Although I did not see her face, I could feel the energy she exuded. Now, it's one thing to be inspired by something, but it's another to put in the work to become it.

I had little money, but I mustered up $39.99 from my welfare check to purchase a blue polyester double-breasted suit from a company called New Port News. Then, I was off to Payless Shoe Source for some black pumps. I had no clue that I should not have paired white stockings with black heels. Don't laugh. That suit represented the woman I was determined to become. Although my self-esteem, confidence, and self-worth were still low, putting on that suit allowed me to see and feel the possibilities of who I could be.

The more I wore the suit, the more my self-concept changed. So much so that when I was not wearing it, I still presented myself as a confident being. Because I only had a silhouette vision of this woman, I had no clue of her personality. I thought about the women I admired, and it hit me. I took on the calm demeanor of Sheryl Lee Ralph's character, Dee, in the sitcom Moesha. Now, I'm still a work in progress, but I have learned to respond versus react. I also loved the class and elegance of Diahann Carroll in her

7

character, Dominique Deveraux, on Dynasty. I studied those ladies, took pieces, and applied them to myself.

The more you practice a skill, the more you master it. Remember that part! Long story short, taking small yet consistent steps played a massive role in my transformation.

Now, let's fast forward to 2020...

When the pandemic hit, it caused everyone to look within. It was like the feminine energy rose and demanded her respect. People were asking themselves, do I like my life? Am I happy in my career? Have I neglected my love life? What will I do next? And the list goes on. The sales of our courses and programs increased by 60%. Women were now forced to stop! It's crazy how it takes a catastrophe to cause us to do a self-evaluation.

Your next level requires a new you. I did a check-in with myself because I could feel it was time to do another identity switch. Don't get me wrong; I love the life I've created. In all honesty, I must acknowledge that I had been playing too small. The goals I needed to accomplish required a different version of me. I had gotten complacent and tried to skirt around the upgrades that needed to be made. This was due to not wanting what I thought were the burdens and responsibilities of my transformation. I remember telling myself, "I don't really need that. I can move to the country, get quiet, and live a peaceful farm life." But my desires for particular things grew, and I could no longer ignore them. Although living on acres of land and owning a family compound has been my goal for several years, it wasn't the right time for that.

After taking a deep breath, I sat down and listed what was not yielding the results I wanted. On the other side of the paper, the big question was, who do you need to become to get what you want? How would this woman live her life? How would she dress? What type of friends would she have? What kind of man would she choose? And the list goes on. As I put pen to paper, it became clear that I had to invest my time, effort, and finances into my change.

When you are at the bottom of your next level, it can feel scary. I had been here before, so I knew what was next. I could feel I had tapped out of my current level. My passion was gone, and I felt restless and unproductive.

Because I believe in how potent the feminine energy is, I allowed myself to embrace what I call the Feminine Surrender Mode. I knew this would be critical to my transformation. You may remember the video I shared about that current state if you are in my All Things Feminine Social Club app. You can download the app in your Apple or Google Play store to watch the replay if you haven't seen it.

Making an identity switch may sound like a big task to you. It's like being given a movie script that you have spent months memorizing, only for the director to tell you they gave you the wrong script. Now that you have the new one, you must immediately become that new character. The old script no longer exists, it's a new movie, and you're on!

Girl, don't get nervous; it will be worth it. If you feel like a switch is too much of a task, ask yourself this, "Does my current identity give me the results that I want?" As I always say, "You never have to listen to a word I share, but your results don't lie." In this book, I will walk you through the steps I took to create a life I absolutely love. Get ready for this glorious ride because you are about to become the woman who gets what she wants.

Her Mindset

Okay, ladies, before we can jump into all the glitz and glamor of becoming the woman you desire, we have to start from the very beginning. Although this process need not take forever, it cannot happen without reconditioning your mind. To become *her*, you must go back to what makes you, well you. You must figure out where your beliefs and values come from. Why do you believe what you believe? Why do you think the way that you do? Why do you perceive things the way you do? You must undergo this because nothing can be created successfully on an unstable foundation.

You will not become the best version of yourself without understanding your current state. This requires a lot of self-reflecting, but it's worth it. There are experiences you have buried in the depths of your mind, and many will come to light when you explore within.

Go as far back as you can, even if painful because it is a part of where your identity stems from. Who are you? What experiences brought you to this point? I had to do a complete 180 to transform my life. Everyone sees the end product, but few people witness the "in progress" version of me.

Growing up, I was taught the opposite of the wisdom I believe and share today. I was raised in a very religious household where I thought my mother was passive, submissive, and feminine but had no boundaries. Because of this, I watched as she married someone who did not value her. In return, I did repeat the pattern.

I not only saw this growing up, but I remember the exact moment I felt there was nothing special about me. I was told, "Don't let anyone tell you what you have is special. Especially what's between your legs. Every other woman has one too." Those words played a huge role in my self-worth and feeling inadequate.

I had little to no confidence, low self-esteem, and I constantly felt out of place. I didn't have the love and affection I needed from my parents, so I went out seeking it.

I was surrounded by people who believed that you keep your problems to yourself, pray about them, and give them to God. But *then what?* This is where I learned that it wasn't okay to communicate my feelings and struggle in silence.

The conditioning that most of us have started from our childhood. This is why you must pluck up what isn't working.

Being told there was nothing special about me was the leading cause of the tragic domino effect of my life. I didn't think I was worthy of better. I didn't even know what better should look like. I had seen no one do "better" in my family or where I was from. I had to create my own blueprint. And to do that, I had to believe I was worthy and unique.

I had to do more than verbalize and believe it; I had to become it. A move like this required me to think and behave like a woman who knows she's worthy of genuine and authentic love, happiness, and success. She wouldn't believe otherwise. That woman knew she could have it all! It was scary at first, but I took the leap.

Once I eliminated the idea of not being special, everything shifted for me. People interacted with me differently because I was more confident. I believed there wasn't anything I couldn't have.

I sit back now and think about how different my life would be had I not dug back into my past and reconditioned myself.

This transformation did not happen overnight, and it took being intentional about who I wanted to be. Every decision I made was with the new version of me in mind. I wouldn't do anything that she wouldn't do. I wouldn't entertain anyone that she wouldn't consider. She was confident, so I was too. She was approachable, so I was too. She was kind, so I was too.

This was a substantial challenge. The old version of you will constantly fight against who you want to become, and it's like a good versus evil battle. Is it scary? YES!

You will feel like you are living a lie. Your subconscious mind will fight you so hard because it doesn't want change. Think about it. You've been programmed with years of experiences that are unfavorable. There may be an emotional attachment to the abandonment from mom, rejection from dad, bullying in school, and the list goes on. Those traumas become the lenses we see through to shape our lives.

Once I understood what was going on, I knew I had to forgive people I would never receive an apology from. This taught me that my healing was for me and not for someone else.

How do you forgive someone for taking your innocence? How do you forgive your fiancé for physically abusing you? Let's not forget walking in on him having sex with another woman two months before your wedding. How do you forgive that? You just do it! You don't wait for closure because closure isn't guaranteed. What is guaranteed is if you hold onto hurt and pain, you will deflect those things on people who don't deserve it. Besides, the woman you're becoming would never give someone that much power over her.

Self-sabotaging is real, and I am sure it's a thing we have all been guilty of in our lives. That's what holding onto hurt causes us to do. The person who brought the pain on us is living a carefree life. Why? Because they decided not to care about what they did to you, and they may not even remember. I know it's easier said than done, but you have the power to release it.

Holding onto past pain and traumas will cause blockages. It blocks us from trusting others because we fear being hurt again. It stops happiness because we become paranoid and skeptical of every kind gesture.

To become, I had to question everything I knew, which brought me to my religion. Don't get me wrong, I believe in a higher power; I just do not practice a particular religion.

15

Poverty and religion went hand and hand with my upbringing. They passed down to me what was passed down to them. I had to be comfortable with going through the cognitive dissonance process. I asked God to show me what was real and not what someone forced upon me.

I had to be okay in knowing that although this would be me going against everything I was supposed to believe, I just didn't believe it anymore.

The people I grew up around reminded me of this story. A lady sat on the top of the roof of her house because her neighborhood had flooded. A man on a boat came to help her, and she told him, "No, it's okay. God got me." A man in a helicopter came and threw down a ladder to help her, and she said, "No, it's okay. God got me." Soon after the helicopter left, the water rose above her home, and she drowned. When she made it to heaven, she said to God, "I believed in you. I thought you had me. Why did you let me die?" God said to her, "I sent two people to save you, and you didn't let them. What else was I supposed to do?"

This was far too familiar. The people around me would pray, ask, then wait. It was as if they thought a blessing would fall out of the sky and land in their laps. After seeing this so much, and nothing changing, I knew I had to do something different. This clearly wasn't working for me or anyone that I knew. Once I became aware of this cycle in my adulthood, my perception changed drastically. Instead of waiting and praying, I told myself that I needed to live as a woman full of abundance.

It became easier for my life to fall in place by addressing my wiring. Our mind is one of, if not the *most* powerful thing we have that we underutilize. We have no problem using our minds to create far-fetched hypothetical situations and planning our arguments in our heads with our spouses, friends, and bosses. However, we have a hard time seeing ourselves having a good life. We even put limitations on ourselves in the one place we have complete freedom, and that's in our imagination.

Life may not always give us what we see as positive outcomes. However, only we can decide how we allow those challenges to affect us. We get to choose how they will shape our minds, which is linked directly to how we will live our lives. Your beliefs create your life. Sit and think about it for a moment. Where you are in life directly connects with your core beliefs. Be it conscious or unconscious.

The same mental energy used to think you can't is the same mental energy you need to believe that you can—no matter what seeds have been planted that say otherwise.

It starts with your mind—the "*what if*" habits you have must cease for you to free yourself. Everyone has seen or heard something that has made them feel less than, inadequate, and even undeserving in their lives. It's safe to say that we have also heard some very encouraging words; we just don't give them much attention.

Many of us are guilty of highlighting the negative rather than the positive. I remember hearing Les Brown say, "It takes hearing positive words spoken over you 17 times to combat the one negative. You must remember you have the power to control your mind; use it! It goes to show how tightly we hold on to the negative.

I would be lying if I said I had no hiccups along the way. Many of them, but I dusted myself off and kept going. If you revert to your older patterns, simply reset yourself.

Questions to Ask Yourself

- Who had the most influence on my childhood and beliefs?

- Do I default to negative thinking when something goes wrong or right?

- Can I see the generational patterns in my life?

- How do I respond when people challenge my beliefs?

- What do I have limiting beliefs about?

- Do I wonder "what if" all the time?

- Do I believe that I am worthy of a better life?

- Am I afraid of success?

Her Femininity

The most important thing I want you to take away from this chapter is that femininity is not pink, nor is it reserved for a man.

Say it with me, ladies *"femininity is not just the color pink nor is it reserved for a man."*

Please throw away any preconceived notions of femininity before picking up this book. Please remain open-minded, as I explain.

Although surrendering is associated with femininity, it is not the way many would assume. When people hear the word femininity, they envision a woman who is only meek, mild, soft-spoken, gentle, and has light energy. However, many also feel that femininity means to be submissive, a doormat, and weak. Femininity is very much assertive, wild, dark, and destructive. She is nurturing yet no-nonsense! Why do you think the earth is described as "Mother Nature?"

"Mother Nature is **a personification of nature that focuses on the life-giving and nurturing aspects of nature by embodying it**, in the form of the mother." - Webster's Dictionary.

Mother Nature is kind, gentle, nurturing, supportive, and provides resources for all. However, she also has a destructive nature to protect herself. Humans have destroyed, mistreated, and vandalized Mother Earth with their plans for centuries. When she pushes back, it's with a vengeance. It does not mean she loses her nurturing motherly traits; she will just destroy anything in her path that is not true.

Now that is an accurate representation of feminine energy. It isn't this or that, but this and that.

Now let's take a little look at history. We've all heard of a woman by the name of Cleopatra. She was a very powerful woman who used her femininity to capture the hearts of Julius Caesar and Mark Anthony. Interestingly enough, she captivated two of the most powerful men of our time, and with many philosophers describing her as not easy on the eyes. This clears up the idea that feminine women have to look like Beyonce or a Kardashian, which couldn't be further from the truth.

Although Cleopatra's physical beauty was not deemed one of her assets, she used femininity, intellect, and charm to her advantage. She spoke several languages, proficient in astronomy, mathematics, economics, politics, and philosophy. When she entered a room, she owned it. She had something that made men want her and women want to be her.

Although she was brilliant, wise, and intelligent, she understood the nature of men. She knew that she could not show only her intelligence to reel in her love interest.

Cleopatra was said to have married her brother to carry on the family lineage. Back then, this was normal behavior. Preserving the family bloodline was mandatory. However, her brother became very greedy and decided that he wanted all the power and wealth.

Because of his greed, he made it his mission to have his sister destroyed by any means necessary. No matter who he sent her way, men could not kill her but instead fell in love with her. Seduction, femininity, and sensuality were her weapons of choice. So much so, she caused wars between kings.

She understood the importance of using her charm, intellect, and luring men into her feminine world. It takes a lot of confidence to move as she did, which tells me she believed in herself. So much so, she left an impact everywhere she set her feet.

Pamela Harriman was considered one of the most charming women of the 20th century. Her secret weapon was her ability to make people, men especially, feel special.

Confidence, intelligence, vulnerability, and understanding men are two things both women have in common.

Pamela Harriman made other people feel special because *she* felt special. She believed she deserved the best and went after it. She gave people what they needed because she was attentive enough to learn what they desired. She could not do this successfully if she was uncertain about herself or making everything about her.

This is why I continue to stress that your femininity is not about getting a man but about you. It will be impossible to have successful romantic or platonic relationships until you make an identity switch and see yourself as someone fabulous and deserving.

I was feminine long before I was aware of it. I didn't know how to use it, nor did I realize that everyone should not have access to certain levels of my femininity. My past experiences caused me to show up in my 'I got it to protect myself' masculine energy. Being molested for 12 years, dealing with two rapes and domestic violence will make you distrust others. It will cause you to barricade your softer side and be on alert constantly. You don't realize that you are living in fear. Then you wonder why others don't genuinely check on you. It's because you have shown them that you are self-contained.

Before we go any further, let me explain that women and men have masculine and feminine energy. Men generally have more of the masculine and women the feminine. So, there is nothing wrong with using that energy when you need it. However, you don't live your life in the masculine energy. Our bodies aren't wired to handle that; this is where the imbalance happens. It's like trying to jump a car; you need the negative and the positive—the yin and yang. Polarity is required in everything.

I am using my masculine energy to write this book. I am focused, determined, disciplined, analytical, and goal-oriented.

The sentiment that a feminine woman is a doormat, weak, agreeable about everything has always been laughable. A wise feminine woman is the complete opposite. She has boundaries, self-love, vulnerability, is gentle with herself, feels her emotions, is in tune with her body, stands up for herself, and the list goes on. A naive feminine woman does not possess that level of awareness. She goes with the flow, doesn't question much, lets men have access to her body with no requirements, and goes against her intuition for pleasing others. She does not check in with her body to see how she's feeling.

Another myth we must dismantle is dressing girly, having your nails done, wearing a dress, heels, and putting on makeup, makes you feminine. Femininity is not a look. Have you ever encountered a woman who looked the part, but her demeanor, attitude, and energy didn't match the look? Did I just describe you?

If I did, it's okay. When you know better, you do better, and it is long overdue to do better. Feminine women compete with no one because there are no competitions.

Here is a motto I live by.

When I walk in the room, there will always be someone prettier than me, have a better body than me, is more educated than me, and has more money than me. But there will NEVER be anyone in a room better than me!

You must be aware of the energy you carry before describing yourself as a feminine woman. Being aware of this will always help you decipher between someone who *is* feminine and someone who *looks* feminine.

Being a feminine woman is a lifestyle. It isn't something that you turn on and off. A feminine woman can be gentle yet powerful and assertive with her words all simultaneously. She is effortlessly herself. She is wise. She knows when to talk and when to listen. She knows when to let others lead as she follows.

She is someone everyone wants to be friends with and get to know. She's mysterious, intriguing, yet personable. She is not competing with anyone other than herself because she always strives to be the best version of herself. She is confident and proud of herself. She is wild, free, and open. She knows and loves who she is at her core.

Understanding who you are at your core helps you unlock your feminine power. It will show you how you are internally wired.

Who are you? Do you know?

Figuring out who you are will allow you to discover your feminine brand. Yes, you have your own brand of femininity. I named my brand "Refined Hood." Although I am a girly girl, I still have a little hood in me, and I am just fine with that. I was raised on the rough side of Richmond, CA, so it's in me, and I am not ashamed of it. However, she comes out when needed, especially if she doesn't feel protected. I love this balance and don't feel less feminine because of it. I had to tame her because she was something else. That's another book.

Another myth I would like to debunk is you must be a petite woman to be feminine. Do not let social media, tv, or anyone else tell you otherwise. Femininity is not a look; it's the soft, gentle, loving, free, compassionate, nurturing, open, sensual energy that speaks from a deeper part of you.

Many people, my daughter included, are not built like the ideal image of what a feminine woman is supposed to look like. In the same way, we have masculine and feminine energy; we have male and feminine features. We are all created from a man and woman. It is not far-fetched to think that many of us may have features from our fathers, but does that make you less feminine? No, it doesn't.

You have no control over your height, hands, skin complexion, foot size, nose, or any other part of your body. This is why your physical features have nothing to do with you being feminine. It's about the type of energy that you fill that body with.

One thing that helped me become more feminine was to allow people to help me in all areas of my life. I had to stop being upset that everyone dumped their burdens on me because I was viewed as the strong friend. I needed to start asking and accepting help. I would either suffer in silence by keeping my issues to myself. Or I would give the illusion I had things under control, even when I didn't.

I am unsure if the fear of embarrassment or my pride wouldn't let other people help me, but I knew whatever I was doing wasn't working. Nobody came to my rescue because no one believed I needed rescuing. I was always trying to figure it out when all I needed was to ask and accept.

If you're a social media follower, you know I love to say that my wrists are broke, especially when men are around. I would have to fall out for someone to believe I needed them, but not anymore! Once I learned the art of accepting help, my life became much more prosperous.

Remember, the woman you want to become does not have this issue. She knows that she cannot do it alone, and she does not want to.

Being a damsel in distress changed my life. I realized more than anything that some people like to be of service to you. Think about it. We feel good when helping others. Why take that away from someone else when it comes to you.

Just because you can handle it yourself doesn't mean you should. I don't care if it's as simple as a young man at Kroger asking if you need help carrying your three grocery bags to your car; say yes! What are you losing from letting someone help you? Nothing.

When you get into the space and energy of receiving from others without feeling weird about it or without feeling like you owe them something in return, that is how you know you are becoming more of a feminine woman. You are learning how to relinquish control.

The art of receiving can feel uncomfortable because we rarely feel like we deserve it. Well, honey, that is the old version of you. The new you know she deserves good things because she is alive. Period! It is tough to receive when you have been accustomed to only giving. But to tap into your true feminine self, you must be able to let other people make your life easier.

Being a mom of three doing it all was a challenge, but it is not an excuse. I had to turn my feminine switch on, and when I finally did, my life changed quickly. Had I known then what I know now, my life would have probably looked different while I was in my 20s, but there is no time limit for this transformation. There is no such thing as it being too soon or too late to become a feminine woman. All that matters is that when your lightbulb finally does come on, you utilize it properly.

On your journey of becoming, you will understand the importance and need for peace, tranquility, gratitude, and happiness.

Questions To Ask Yourself

- What brand of femininity would the woman I am becoming have?

- Do I operate in more of my masculinity or femininity? In what areas?

- When you think of a feminine woman, who comes to mind?

- Am I okay with letting go of control?

- Do I know how to allow people to help me?

- How do I feel about being a damsel in distress?

- Am I approachable?

- Do you hear "smile beautiful"?

- Do people check on me?

Her Habits

Now, ladies, this chapter goes hand in hand with the first chapter, Her Mindset. Once you have reprogrammed and rewired your mind, your habits must also be aligned. Not just in some areas, but in all areas. Your habits play a massive role in the direction your life will take.

Before I understood the importance of creating positive habits, I didn't realize I already had some bad ones. I was an emotional eater, workaholic, and I reacted instead of taking a moment to think and respond.

Being an entrepreneur also played a role in why I did not create the best habits. I wasn't coming home at the same time every day from work. I was the work. My life probably would have been less chaotic if I did work a typical 9-5. I tried that, but it just didn't work for me.

I was a robot, and a slave to my business. I gave my children the necessities like food, shelter, clothes, and water. I couldn't be more present because I was always trying to do more to keep a roof over our heads. Yes, it paid off in the long run, but at the expense of not bonding with my children when they were smaller. I didn't understand the power of simply making my bed when I woke up in the morning. I had to learn how to slow down and take the time to be intentional about my day. Do you know that simply making your bed every day changes everything?

I am not sure if you've ever noticed, but a different feeling comes over you when you come home to a clean home.

When you create positive habits, those habits transfer over to other areas of your life. If you are always on the go and hustling and grinding, you probably move in this fashion when you go out. You don't give people a chance to know you because you don't sit down long enough to be noticed.

If you're always on the go, it is also likely that you are always in a rush when you go grocery shopping, and you don't even know why. This takes away our ability to enjoy moments because we never actually stay in them long enough.

What does this have to do with making your bed every day? Everything! Getting in the habit of making your bed every morning prompts you to slow down before starting your day. It takes less than 10 minutes to make up your bed and, in return, you feel more relaxed when you come home.

Have you ever noticed that you have difficulty being productive when your home is cluttered? Your home reflects what's going on inside of you. A cluttered mind can bring a disorderly house. This is another reason it is essential to slow down and be intentional about your actions.

If you don't have any positive habits, you need to create them today. Aside from making your bed every day, I suggest you start with meditating, a morning and night routine, maintaining a hobby, and telling Jessica to shut the hell up. Don't worry; I'll explain who she is later.

Being still and meditating is one activity I love.

Meditating teaches you how to tap into your inner self. It teaches you to concentrate and disconnect from things that don't matter even if it is only for a short moment.

Meditating brings peace and tranquility. This is the energy you should be in so you can manifest, but that's a different conversation. Meditating helps heal areas of your body thrown out of whack due to traumas.

Having a morning and night routine is mandatory. You absolutely cannot go to sleep and wake up any kind of way. The way you go to bed can affect the morning you will have, which also plays a role in how the next day will start. Do you see how this is all connected?

Making your bed in the morning can be part of your morning routine. Your night routine starts your cycle. Have you ever gone to sleep upset, and when you woke up, you were still in a janky mood, but you didn't know why? Your body didn't forget how it felt before you closed your eyes. You must get into a habit of taking care of her.

Something I love to do that allows me to wake up and sleep better at night is sleeping in lingerie. You have to get out of the habit of thinking that lingerie is for a man. Lingerie is for you first.

Lingerie makes you feel sexy naturally. The material and the design alone turn you into a vixen. I dare you to go to sleep in lingerie and wake up with an attitude. When you put on lingerie, your mood changes, and you instantly become more sensual.

You oil your body gentler, your energy becomes softer, and you feel even more beautiful than you already are. This is how you should feel after having a long day.

Now, I am not saying you need to wear lingerie every day, but I am saying you should be doing things that allow you to relax and wind down. Take a bubble bath. Light candles and listen to music when you get out of the shower. Wash your face. Take a shower in the dark with just a candle for light. Get in the habit of doing something that reminds you to calm down and relax.

When you get into the habit of doing this, you are also practicing regular self-maintenance. If you are single, this will be a part of who you are and not who you're trying to be for someone else. If you're married, put yourself first in this manner, and your husband will notice.

Going to bed feeling flustered and overwhelmed does nothing but spill over into the next day. It causes a never-ending cycle of restlessness because you're not adequately winding down nightly. You're rushing in the morning, hence moving fast and not making your bed when you wake up. Do you get it? I think you do.

Another essential habit is having a hobby. A few things I enjoy doing are pottery painting and picking flowers.

Living a life you enjoy is imperative to your happiness. Having a hobby doesn't always have to be done outside your home. However, it should cause you to step away from your phone. I don't care what your hobby is; make time for it and create a life worth living.

Now let's talk about the infamous Jessica. Jessica is my negative old basic mindset. I gave her a name I could identify when the negative self-talk, sabotage, and doubting myself would show up. You can give yours a name as well. On my journey to becoming a woman who gets what she wants, I kept having battles between the woman I was and the woman I was transforming into. Jessica made sure she was around to remind me of my older beliefs.

I struggled with Jessica because my new way of being was something Jessica (AKA my subconscious mind) was not familiar with. This caused a major war within because self-doubt would kick in every time I took an unfamiliar step.

Before I became who I am today, I would constantly compare myself to other people, especially women. "*Why are you going to this event? You are nothing like them.*" "*You come from poverty. You can't afford to gamble on starting a business.*" "*You should have done this when you were younger; it won't work now.*" "*You have three kids. You don't have time to date.*"

Those are all the thoughts Jessica would say every time I would try to do something out of the norm. Every time I gave myself grace. Every time I mustered up hope, here she comes telling me to be more realistic. I had to learn how to control and silence her.

The moves you make are bound to be scary, and they are supposed to be. You are being stretched, and you must endure the emotional pain that comes with change. Are you ready for that?

There is no growth in comfort. You will have many situations where you get scared, but you can't allow that to stop you from moving forward. The unknown is a terrifying place because you are no longer in control. However, staying stuck is not an option.

Girl, listen. Jessica will bully you into staying the same. Put her in her place, and fast! She can only give you your current results. Is that what you want?

The biggest lesson you will gain once you learn how to push out the negative and walk toward the positive is the ability to trust yourself truly.

We often end up in predicaments because we do not trust our intuition. We don't trust ourselves or our decision-making.

We can be indecisive, overthink, and make the same mistakes. We even go against that inner tug trying to guide us. We believe the outside world knows best for us, instead of the beautiful GPS called intuition that the creator gave us.

As you go through this identity switch, it will become easier to decipher your intuition from fear. It can feel the same, so pay attention to what's going on inside you. You will know its fear when you examine the situation, and you are not in harm's way. When you realize nothing terrible is happening, you don't want to leave your comfort zone.

This does not happen overnight, and it will require daily repetition. You start by trusting your intuition with small things. When you do this, you are working your trust muscle. It can seem insignificant but do not discount it. I often tell the story about how one Thanksgiving, I was ill, but the kids wanted Hawaiian rolls. When I sat in the car, my intuition told me to drive about 5 miles to the bread store, but April, doing what she wanted to do, went 2 minutes away to a packed Walmart.

I'm sure you can guess how that went. No rolls! Once again, that nudging led me to the bread store. I headed that way after kicking and screaming because I didn't want to drive. To my surprise, the store was stocked with Hawaiian rolls.

This is what I mean by practicing trusting yourself with small things.

Creating a habit of shutting Jessica up will help you fight against any negative commentary drowning out your intuition. This includes those who do not understand this transformation you're embarking on.

Questions to Ask Yourself

- What type of morning and night routine would the woman I'm becoming have?

- What hobbies interest me?

- Do I hold myself accountable?

- What is my go-to when I am stressed?

- Am I an emotional eater?

- Do I like to participate in safe activities?

- What are two bad habits I will replace with productive habits for a least 30 days?

Her Standards

noun

plural noun: **standards**

   1. 1.

   a level of quality or attainment.

   "their restaurant offers a high standard of service."

Throughout my career of working with thousands of women, I would ask, what is your standard? What would that look like? The answer would sound something like this: "He has to have a degree, God-fearing, have a car, own living quarters, make six figures... blah, blah, blah!"

I hate to be the bearer of bad news, but if that is your standard, you're already losing. When I speak of standards, I'm talking about for your life. Please believe that the woman you want to become has one.

In a nutshell, the standard you have for your life will determine how other people will treat you and what you will accept. This is not just limited to a romantic relationship. It's your standard of living based on your level of self-esteem and what you believe you deserve.

If you look at your life now, are you happy and content with where you are? If not, it's due to the value you have for yourself. This may be hard to hear, but you probably don't love yourself the way you think you do.

When you love yourself, and I mean really love yourself, you don't play about you, honey. You don't play about your self-care, appearance, peace, energy, and anything else about you.

If you've ever had to sell yourself to someone on why you are unique, you don't value or love yourself *enough*. You should never have to explain your worth to anyone. As the saying goes, "if you have to sell someone on you, you will have to always sell them on why they should keep you."

Your value for yourself is displayed through your actions and how you make decisions. This is why it is crucial to work on your self-esteem and confidence before building any platonic or romantic relationship.

People can sense when someone does not value themselves, and this is how we end up with stories about people using and doing us wrong. When you love yourself *enough,* you can sense when someone is being disingenuous because you are more focused on having people around you who would complement or add to the love you have for yourself.

As many of you know, my daughter was married and is now divorced. When I met her ex-husband, I told her he wasn't the one, and I knew this because he had a conversation with her about how easy it is for people to get over on her.

He tried to frame it as though he identified her weakness and wanted to protect her from others, but I knew he was preying on my child. Although she was put together financially, he could sense she was naïve.

This is why it is essential to make sure that the version of yourself you're presenting to the world is the version that loves herself so much she can sense when she is being preyed on.

It becomes easy to be mistreated, mishandled, and underappreciated when you don't love yourself. You must have standards and boundaries for yourself before you can ever have standards for anything else.

This is not to excuse people who use and abuse good people, but we don't control what people do; we only control what we allow. This is another reason it's essential to have standards and know what you should and should not accept.

If you wouldn't let others talk to you with disrespect, don't speak to yourself with disrespect.

How often do you make a mistake and say, "I'm so stupid, I don't know why I just did that," or "I'm dumb, my bad"? From this day forward, talking to yourself like that is unacceptable. If you wouldn't let someone else speak to you in that manner, why would you say that to yourself?

You may not mean it in the way it's being said; however, those thoughts shouldn't come to mind at all when you speak of yourself. You are human and should have high self-esteem, love, and respect for who you are so you do not use harmful speech towards yourself.

If you notice you are speaking to yourself in a manner that would offend you if someone else talked to you that way, correct it immediately.

We have been conditioned not to like or love ourselves. This is why we are afraid to set a solid standard. We give people passes and accept poor treatment sacrificing ourselves.

Remember, you train people on how to treat you. Self-love affirmations can help you. Here are a few of my favorite:

I am loved

I am enough

I am beautiful

I am worthy

I belong

I am confident

I am unique

I deserve the best

I can do this

I am peace

I am light

When you repeat positive affirmations enough, you eventually believe them. Even if you have to grab sticky notes and put them all over your house or set reminders on your phone to recite a few of these a day, do what you have to do so these thoughts will become a part of your DNA.

When you make a mistake, you'll remember to give yourself grace. When things get hard, you'll remember to handle yourself with care. That's when you'll feel the shift between how you loved yourself before and how you love yourself now.

You are becoming the type of woman who has a standard of "I can be, do and have whatever I want."

When you experience this self-love and confidence, your life will change. Everyone will be forced to treat you like a new person, which they should because you are.

The new you will require you to hold yourself accountable. Your standards in one area of your life will usually spread across all areas. You cannot pick and choose when to apply them.

That's how you know that your standards have become part of your DNA and a way of life. Like I said earlier, you can't control what people say and do to you, but you can always choose what you entertain. Just because you have new standards doesn't mean that people like you will only approach you. Everyone is attracted to the light.

The new you will help you identify who you should and should not entertain. You can identify insecurities and issues you once had to overcome, which will allow you to understand how you should handle them.

Identifying these traits in people is a huge indicator you align with yourself because you are less likely to be blindsided by people the way you used to be. No matter how much work you do on yourself, you will run into people on lower frequencies, but that is not a direct reflection of you. Although light attracts everything, you will notice you will meet more people like you.

Remember: You are not responsible for what you attract, but you are responsible for what you entertain, and it is a direct reflection of what you are aligned with.

Most of the time, to know how much you have grown and healed, you pay attention to the people coming toward you the most.

This does not mean you haven't made progress, but it's the reality. When people can see the beautiful light in you, they want to get close to it. It's your job to use those standards to determine if they qualify.

This goes for platonic friendships and relationships. I am sure most of us have experienced having a toxic friend, coworker, and even family members. Surround yourself with people—male and female—who hold standards for themselves. Friends like these will hold you accountable as well when they see you slipping.

Always be very selective with who you share your energy with. As I continue to express, people are attracted to light energy, but the wrong people can suck this energy out of you, so not everyone should get access.

The company you keep and the people you entertain should reflect positively on the standards you hold for yourself. If you ever find that they don't, you need to refer to this chapter and reset those standards by any means necessary.

Questions to Ask Yourself

- What kind of standards would the woman you're becoming have?

- What type of results have I gotten with my current standards?

- What area of my life am I struggling in the most?

- What pattern have I noticed with my friendships?

- What pattern have I noticed with my relationships?

- Am I a nice girl who accepts whatever comes her way?

- Do I have weak boundaries?

- What can I do now to elevate my standards?

Her Environment

Raise your hand if your car is clean right now. I mean at this very moment. What about the junk drawer in the kitchen? If you have a shameful smirk on your face, it's okay. A few years ago, I wouldn't have been able to raise my hand either. I used to be in such a rush I didn't have time to keep my car clean regularly. The junk drawer was my personal "I promise I will read it later" hoarding location.

I didn't realize how I kept my environment reflected what was going on inside. It wasn't until I paid more attention to my home and work life I understood why I was always carrying such a heavy and rushed energy everywhere I would go.

Some say that women keep their cars, closets, and rooms a mess. There are a few exceptions to the rule, but if I'm being honest, I would have to say I believe this to be true. Our rooms and closets usually have clothes, shoes, papers, and makeup everywhere.

We need to handle this because it creates a habit of living in clutter, which is not healthy or helpful to our everyday lives. No matter how busy we are, we must be aware of our environment. You are more likely to thrive in clean environments because it brings clarity.

I have created some of my most remarkable work in a clean environment, and I have procrastinated the most in a cluttered environment.

If your car and home are cluttered, I can bet that your cubicle or office is cluttered. Let's talk about that snack drawer at the office. If you've ever been where you've had an unexpected guest and had to hurry up and clean before they arrived, this chapter is for you.

So, let's talk about one main reason we have a lot of clutter in our environment. Are you ready for this? Here it is. Our environment is an outward manifestation of what is happening on the inside. Yep, I had to learn this the hard way. We become robotic in our day-to-day routine, and we do not stop and check in with ourselves.

I remember when I first had that ah-ha moment. One day, guests had come into town unexpectedly and wanted to stop by. My home was not prepared for company, and I had been feeling blah for a few weeks. What did I do? I made myself presentable and stuffed everything in closets, drawers, and under the bed. My home was lovely and tidy, just don't open the hall closet door.

After my guest left, it hit me that my issues were internal. It was deeper than an unkept house; I was dealing with depression and didn't know it. You must give some much-needed attention to your mental and emotional health. Tune in to the feelings and experiences that need addressing. Doing this will allow you to clean and organize the physical clutter around you.

Your lifestyle is created by whatever type of environment you make. We will talk about your lifestyle later in the book, but your environment plays a massive role in what you're manifesting for your life. Your home is also your healing space.

Once I took care of my mental and emotional health, it was time to get my surroundings in order. For me, this also meant being more aware.

So, what would the woman I wanted to become do? She hires a maid, a chef, uses Instacart to pick her groceries, and brings in a professional organizer. So that is precisely what I did. No matter your budget, implement what you can afford. I even started putting things back in their proper place because I was notorious for leaving the top off of bottles. It became second nature to the point if I didn't close a cabinet all the way, my mind would remind me to go back and do so.

The type of woman I wanted to become had a very peaceful and welcoming palace. So once again, I created that, and I researched on YouTube how to do just that.

When anyone visits my home, they express how peaceful and calm they feel. That is the serenity and aura I intentionally created for my home. I desired to make my home a Zen place for myself and anyone I invited. This meant I had to become peace and serenity within myself. Do you see how that all comes together?

A few years ago, I announced to my social media supporters I was diagnosed with Lupus. Dealing with this made it even more apparent how important it was to create a stress-free environment because it kept me from having flare-ups. I later found out that mental, emotional, and physical stress brought on the autoimmune disease. My body and mind were in survival mode for many years. I'm glad I caught it when I did. However, I wonder if I could have avoided it had I been more at peace.

Having a tranquil, clean, and clear environment allows me to sleep better. Sleep is a big part of my beauty regimen.

My Zen environment has trickled over into our business headquarters as well. We had our grand opening earlier this year, and across the board, we heard how peaceful it felt inside. The guests assumed that the event planner helped decorate the building, and they were surprised to know that all she provided was the balloons, table décor, and food.

I decorated my office building myself. All the blush, mauve, faux carpets, old Hollywood glam, and softness is a representation of the woman I had become. If you ask my mom, she will tell you how I always wore dark colors, had dark furniture, and was just an overall dark person growing up. I didn't want to be seen. Well, the woman I became had no problem showing up in the world just as fabulous as she wanted to be.

My home and headquarters inspire me and increase my creativity because it's hard not to be inspired in a peaceful environment.

I can't express enough what changing your environment will mentally, financially, spiritually, and emotionally do for you. You don't always have to relocate either; you can do a complete transformation at your current residence. Check out Pinterest and YouTube for inspiration. If you relocate, you will get the same results if you haven't dealt with the clutter of your heart.

Another thing I did was go through each closet, drawer, and garage to get rid of items that no longer served me. If you are short on cash, this is a great way to make some extra. It was embarrassing how I accumulated so much stuff during the height of the pandemic. Amazon was my best friend.

What in the world did I need with a rice cooker? Since when did I not know how to make fluffy rice with a pot on the stove? See, I was trying to be fancy unnecessarily. At the end of it all, you must decide what type of environment the woman you desire to become would surround herself with. This includes the places she goes and the company she keeps. It will feel weird because it is supposed to! You are no longer the old you. Have fun with it and enjoy the process.

Questions to Ask Yourself

- What type of environment would the woman I desire to be created?

- What emotional issues have I suppressed?

- Are my mind and emotions cluttered?

- Do I struggle with throwing things away?

- What can I do to create a peaceful home environment?

- What area of my home should I organize first?

Her Style

Although being a feminine woman is about so much more than wearing cute clothes and expensive shoes, how you dress plays a huge role in how you feel, and how others will address you. Just because you're a feminine woman doesn't mean your favorite colors are pastels.

I was not too fond of pink or anything soft for a while. It took me some time to find my style, and once I did, I stuck with it.

You must find your signature look. There isn't a right or wrong style, but you must ask yourself, would the woman I want to become dress this way? Does my current style give me the results that I'm after? Everything you do, including what you wear, should be funneled through the eyes of the woman you want to become. You may believe your current style is impressive, but there is one question. Is it getting you the response you want?

It's hard to hear someone tell you that your style may need to change. Listen, beautiful, you are not average, and everything you wear should complement your body and personality. Anything that does not make you look like a ten needs to be given away or sold.

The woman you want to become would never be caught out in the world looking like she just threw something on. She takes pride in how she shows up.

Your style will affect how people *see* you before you open your mouth. I know what you're saying, "people should not judge you by your appearance." In all honesty, that is not the world we live in. We want to think that we don't judge others in this way, but we do.

You don't have to buy designer clothes, but I recommend purchasing quality clothes. Pieces that will last a long time. I am a big fan of dresses that have a lining in them. They give a polished appearance. I am also a big fan of a sundress. I wear them around the house all year round. I will also have my seamstress add a breathable lining to a few.

Before we go any further, I need to express this to you. Do not compare yourself to another woman. I need you to really get this. It is ok to be inspired by another woman's style; remember to bring your uniqueness to that style.

Your style should combine what you *like* and what *looks good* on you. Sometimes what we want looks better on the mannequin than on us.

The most beautiful thing about being a woman is that we come in different shapes and sizes. Part of what makes your style your style is owning your body. Not being ashamed of what you don't have, but instead embracing what you do have.

Although I have hips, I often speak about not having a butt. I have a coke bottle shape but no hump in the back. It's not an issue unless I make it an issue. Could I go and get a BBL? Sure. Or I can embrace what I have and wear clothing that enhances the other parts of my body I love instead of focusing on the ones I lack.

I love my hips, shoulders, neckline, and chest. So, guess what? I buy clothes that enhance those things. Everyone knows that I love to wear off-the-shoulder shirts and dresses. That has been my signature look since the 10th grade.

Now, I still buy clothing to enhance the areas of my body that aren't so great too. Specific leggings, dresses, and pants that make me look like I have something going on back there. I buy them because that makes me feel good too.

I must clarify, there is a big difference between enhancing what you are ashamed of and improving what you have already embraced. The most significant difference between the two is your confidence.

No outfit will look good on you until you have confidence. You don't have to have a perfect body to love your body, but you must have the confidence to love your body so the clothes you choose can love you back.

If you have long legs, wear clothes that show them off. If you have a nice butt, wear clothes that show that off too. You don't have to be half-naked to show off your assets. Buying clothes that enhance your butt, legs, shoulders, or whatever part of your body doesn't require revealing anything but fitting correctly in the right areas.

If you have a long torso, you probably look good in high waist pants than someone who doesn't. I am 5'4 on a good day, and there are items I would love to wear, but they will not work on my body frame.

You need to toss out any clothes that are loose, oversized, faded, dingy looking, or do not fit your body correctly. It doesn't matter how much the outfit means to you or how much of a bargain you got it for; it must go. There should be no clothes in your closet that do not compliment your figure. This includes shoes as well. A quality shoe is a must.

As women, we will buy or keep clothes for the size we want to be one day. There is nothing wrong with having a goal, but let's embrace the now.

The first step in identifying your style is knowing your body shape. Please see the diagram below.

WOMEN'S BODY SHAPES

TRIANGLE	RECTANGLE	APPLE	HOURGLASS	PEAR

Once you have done this, I recommend setting up an appointment with a style consultant. This can be done virtually or in person. If you have a Bloomingdale's in your area, set up a 90-minute no-obligation consultation. Another one of my favorite places is Anne Fontaine. I'm obsessed with her clothing and how helpful and friendly the staff has always been, no matter the location. You can also find a stylist who can assist you virtually. Instagram is a great place to do your research. Try using the hashtag #virtualstylist. Pinterest is also excellent for gathering fashion ideas. Just remember, this step will pull you out of your comfort zone. Yes, it is supposed to feel weird, but go for it anyway!

Now let's talk about the proper underwear and shapewear. My grandmother taught us always to wear shapewear no matter our size when I was a teenager. She was about 5'9 and a slender woman. She believed it made a woman look more refined. I would have to agree with her.

A woman should have a drawer filled with shapewear for any occasion. Think about the type of events the woman you want to become would attend. Dinner parties, charity events, social events, vacations, dates, etc. What kind of undergarments would she need to own to ensure she looks exquisite?

Are you getting excited? Can you imagine what your new life will look like? Good, now let's move on to bras.

Even if it is only by two inches, wearing a bra too big can make your breast sag and not feel secure. Have you ever had to constantly pull up your bra through your clothes when you were out? Or constantly shifting your breast inside your bra to ensure they are sitting right? What about having to continually check to make sure the wire isn't poking out? Yeah, throw it away.

It's challenging to find the right bra for you. The best thing I could have ever done was have a bra fitting at JCPenney's. If they still offer them, I highly recommend it. Just as with shapewear, you must have a variety of bras. Because I wear off-the-shoulder clothing often and I am busty, I'm frequently asked, what is my strapless bra secret? Here it is. I purchase them a size smaller. Yep, that is my secret. Once I find a brand I love, I go for a smaller size. It holds and pushes the girls up fabulously.

How we show up in the world reflects how we feel about ourselves. Your style will always make a statement, but it is up to you to choose the statement you want the world to receive.

Questions to Ask Yourself

- What style would the woman I want to become have?

- Does my current style represent who I desire to be?

- Have I embraced my body in its current state? Why or why not?

- How do I want to be viewed by others?

- What fashionista am I inspired by?

- When was the last time, if ever have I've been adequately measured? (bust, waist, hips, chest, arms, etc.)

- Am I willing to let go of clothing that does not serve me?

- Will I commit to having some of my clothes tailored?

- What color compliments my skin the most?

- What is my body shape?

- When was the last time I went shopping?

- Do I like what I see when I stand naked in the mirror? Why or why not?

Her Friendships

The woman you desire to be will have some fantastic friends. To have great friendships, you must first be a great friend. If you say you don't get along with women or "*vibe*" better with men, maybe some healing and better judgment in choosing friends need to happen.

Don't get me wrong; there is nothing wrong with getting along with men. Some of my closest friends are men, but it's not because I don't like or get along with other women. Or vice versa. The men in my life look out for me as a sister, which holds significant weight. Considering I didn't have that type of protection after my grandfather died when I was in the 7th grade.

I treasure the women in my circle. I either went to high school with them or we met along my journey. They have been some of the most loyal and solid women in my life. I have a lot of seasoned women around me as well. I enjoy being in the presence of older wise women. I crave that.

I had to learn to allow women to support me. Just like you, I was very distrusting due to my past experiences. This does not mean you won't attract takers, envy, or jealousy. It happens especially if you have a giving spirit.

However, it doesn't mean you close yourself off from meaningful and reciprocal relationships. The woman you are becoming has boundaries she asserts in her friendships. One of the most attractive things about a woman is her energy and how she carries herself. This isn't just attractive to men, but women as well.

Have you ever been around a southern or older lady, and she called you names like baby, honey, sweetie, or sugar? You usually immediately feel safe around her. Her energy makes you feel comfortable and like you can talk to her about anything.

As many of you know, I call everyone darling. That's just one of my favorite words to use whether I'm talking to men or women. I notice it makes people smile and let their guard down every time.

If you think about it, we smile harder when we receive a compliment from a woman. Maybe it's because we expect men to give them, so when they do, it's nice, but it's not shocking. When women compliment you, it usually comes from a place of genuineness, primarily because we have been trained to compete with one another.

A woman being able to compliment another woman says a lot about her. She is not in competition with you, and she gives credit where credit is due. It is more likely that you would want to get to know her.

Are you ready to look within? Are you friendly? Approachable? Do you have a resting b*tch face? You don't have to be extremely bubbly, but your energy and demeanor will always speak louder than your words ever could. Remember, you're thinking about how the woman you want to become would present herself.

Friendship is about quality, not quantity. Some friendships are forever, and some are seasonal. It's your job to decipher between the two.

We also must hold ourselves accountable for the people we allow in our lives. Many of our decisions are influenced by those closest to us—our family and friends.

Show me your friends, and I'll show you your future.

The friends you keep around are a direct reflection of you. I know that some people may or may not believe the saying, *"Birds of a feather flock together,"* but I think it's an accurate saying when it comes down to your way of life and being.

Therefore, having people in your life that are on the same page as you—especially when it comes to your values and beliefs—is critical to your wellbeing. It is unhealthy to be the smartest or wealthiest friend in your circle. Always be around people you can pour into, and they can pour into you.

If you make this mistake, and most of us have, in being friends with someone who needs you more than you need them or who come to you for everything, but you can't come to them for anything, they can quickly become a spiritual vampire, whether they intend to or not.

Suppose you've ever been friends with someone, and every time you talk to them, you feel exasperated and exhausted from just a conversation. In that case, it is because they're sucking the life out of you, and you are unconsciously soaking in all their problems. They eventually consume you—a spiritual vampire.

The old you would think you're a good friend by listening. As I stated earlier, the new you has boundaries, and she would protect her peace. Which means your circle must be healthy. Make it a point to only surround yourself with people who inspire you, encourage you, and hold you accountable.

There should never be any shade, jealousy, gossiping, or competition, but that starts with you and not them. If you are around people who throw shade, it's usually because that's how you are at your core. You feel comfortable in that environment, and you need to work on that.

When you have true friendships, you don't have to worry about whether someone is making social media posts about you, sharing your private conversations, or talking about you behind your back.

Every romantic and platonic relationship you have is nothing more than a reflection of you. To receive the type of loving, healthy, stable, loyal friendship you desire, you must be that type of friend to others.

Let me warn you; your identity switch may require you to make new friends. Everyone will not understand the new you, and that's ok. If this happens, be ok with making new friends. I know, here I go making you uncomfortable again.

If you aren't extraverted like me, start by asking a woman for help. For instance, if you are in the store trying on clothes, ask for her opinion. It doesn't matter what you need help with; you'll be surprised at how many women are eager and excited to help other women in any way they can.

I enjoy going to the movies, concerts, and even to dinner alone. But the thing about me is, I talk to people everywhere I go. If I'm standing in line at the grocery store, I make conversation with the person next to me. You'll be surprised at who you're standing next to.

I have met so many millionaires, stylists, authors, and people in the same sphere of influence as me by simply saying, hey! It hurts no one to be friendly, and once you are, people tell you about themselves, their life, and their background. This is another reason I treat every person I meet with kindness: you never know what they are going through and how just your presence can bring them comfort.

I remember when my daughter was ten years old and sitting in the backseat of the car. I saw her staring out the window and making faces. I eventually asked her what she was doing, and she shared how rude and annoying it was for the girl in the other car to do that. I then asked, *"How do you know she wasn't staring at you because she thought you were pretty?"* I could tell she hadn't even considered that as a possibility, but it was very much a one.

We have to make sure that when trying to make friends, we are not making our new friends pay for any past mistakes of our old friends. I am not sure why my daughter automatically assumed the worst at ten years old, but that's what we sometimes do.

Therefore, it is imperative to check ourselves before asking for these amazing friends. The last thing you want to do is scare them off with your insecurities. Believe it or not, there are women on the same journey as you looking for authentic friendships.

I lost friends and associates along the way, but I have different friends for different reasons, which has helped my life in so many ways. I have a friend I go to when I am looking to be motivated, need to talk business, spirituality, men, and a friend to go out and cut up with.

The most important thing to remember when building long-lasting and healthy friendships is that one person may not fit all your needs, and it doesn't make them a bad friend. It makes them human. Remember that even your most loyal friends will have slip-ups. Just because someone is a good friend doesn't mean they're the perfect friend.

Surround yourself with people who will value you, uplift you, remind you of your dopeness, and be there for you when you need it. The only thing required for you to meet and make these types of friends is you being this type of friend.

Reciprocity is everything.

- What type of friends does that woman I want to become have?

- What type of friends would the woman I'm becoming have?

- Am I holding onto any toxic friendships?

- Am I the toxic friend?

- When was the last time I told my friends I love, appreciate, or am proud of them?

- Do I feel uncomfortable when I have to console my friends?

- Am I the type of friend I would want to have?

- Do my friends come to me for wise counsel?

- Do my friends make me feel appreciated and cared for?

- Do I think any of my friends are secretly jealous of me?

- Am I secretly jealous of any of my friends?

- Do I ghost my friends when I get into relationships?

Her Money

I remember the days when I struggled hard in the area of finances. I lived in a high-end residential district of Atlanta, Georgia, and was broke. I was so broke, I remember taking toilet paper from the library bathroom because it had gotten that bad.

I was barely making it, not much furniture, but I wanted my children to attend better schools. Although I was struggling, I was in an area full of inspiration. This area would be considered the Beverly Hills of Atlanta. I would drive past the beautiful mansions and imagine myself there.

While the kids were at school, I sat at Whole Foods to work on my business. I would meet businessmen who would sit and share strategies with me. I watched successful women drive away in luxury cars, which motivated me. People did not know that during this time that I was a full-time entrepreneur. Business just wasn't doing well. I was still moving forward, but it seemed like I could never catch a break. I was still teaching entrepreneur classes.

One of the most embarrassing moments of my life was when my car was repossessed in the middle of a conference I was hosting. What made it so bad was, the repo guys walked in smelling like cigarettes and asked me to clean out my car. Well, guess where my car was parked? Right in front of the enormous window, and every conference attendee had a clear view. It broke my heart to talk about being a successful entrepreneur while having my car towed away.

It's no secret that rough patches happen in business, but man, that broke me all the way down. It caused me to get so frustrated that I was forced to make a shift. Why couldn't I drive a luxury car like the ladies at Whole Foods? Why did my apartment have to be scarcely furnished?

I knew it was time for me to become the woman who had her finances in order to stand up. The woman who could buy what she wanted when she wanted. The woman who would never be humiliated because of the lack of money ever again.

It took me some time to realize it, but the reason I had financial issues had everything to do with my perception of money and my upbringing. I didn't grow up seeing people flourish in wealth. I saw people always praying and waiting for it, so I guess that's what I was doing.

I didn't have the degrees and credentials like most people I knew, but I was still a knowledgeable young woman. I had been in the presence of wise people who taught me how to do more than survive. I just had to listen.

I realized that I was too focused on the money, or the lack thereof, and not enough on being the solution to a problem. When you solve problems and bring value, you are never broke.

I had to take the time to understand what my God-given unique gifts were. My skills had nothing to do with "*working hard*" or being a "*go-getter*," but understanding I was already equipped with everything I needed to make the money I wanted to make.

Learning how to manifest played a massive role in my identity switch. It was hard to believe that I could become this woman living in luxury when my car was repossessed, and my bills fell behind. I had to stop paying attention to what was happening around me and focus on my desires. This is precisely what it means to make an identity switch. You go from this to that because you are fed up with the old results.

Once I acted as if everything would be okay, they became okay. Whenever a bill came up, and I knew I didn't have the money to pay for it, it would always show up. I learned the Law of Assumption from a philosopher named Neville Goddard. His teachings changed my way of being.

The reason people have such a hard time manifesting money and love is because of the emotional attachment we have toward them. The more you want it, the less likely you'll have it.

I know it sounds backward but think about it. When you apply for a job, and you know you did well on the interview, you walk away confidently believing, "Yeah, that job is mine," and then you go on about your day.

Do you know why you do this? Because you believe it's already yours. You're not stressing over it. And you're not impatiently waiting for a response because you know it's meant for you.

Money will always come to me because I believe I was not born to just struggle. I didn't believe this until I started my gift basket business, and I charged $50, and the customer gave me $125 and told me not to lowball myself. This is how I learned I had to align with the energy of financial abundance. It taught me to value the gifts I bring to the world and put a price tag on them. You cannot be compensated for what you're worth because you are priceless. However, you can be paid for the results you provide.

There is no way we, as women, are the creators of life but have a problem creating money on demand. This should be something we come out of the womb knowing how to do, but it's hard to do when you have responsibilities that keep you from tapping into this side of you.

It usually takes us a while to truly understand this, but we are money magnets. It's not just an affirmation but a fact. The only reason we have a hard time initially attracting the money floating around us is that we don't believe it exists or that we deserve it.

As I have said often and will continue to say throughout this book, your mentality is the starting point to everything.

You will not become a woman with her finances in order if you don't own that belief.

One of the most significant conflicts people have with thinking like this is that it goes against what we've been told about money. Since childhood, most of us have been told that you must work hard to get it, money doesn't go on trees, and to live from paycheck to paycheck as well as, without struggle, you won't know how to appreciate money.

I couldn't disagree more with this way of conditioning.

I've learned that you don't have to go through hell to appreciate peace. You can just have peace. You shouldn't have to struggle to appreciate your success. And you shouldn't have to work so hard to get something that has always been waiting for you to take it.

The only requirements to becoming a financially abundant woman are changing how you view yourself, dismantle your old beliefs about money, know that you are worthy, and tap into your natural gifts and talents. Understanding your gift and your purpose to the world will attract money to you.

Also, the woman you are becoming has a portfolio full of assets and investments. She doesn't just think for today but also for her legacy. Even though your financial status may not be where you would like, make an appointment with a financial advisor for guidance on where to start.

You should be excited right now because the sky is the limit for you. Your old identity was wrapped in lack and struggling. Honey, those days are over.

Your job is to create a place for this version of you to exist. You will never have to work hard to earn money when you do this because it will always be ready and available to you.

It's waiting on this version of you to show up now.

Questions to Ask Yourself

- What is the financial status of the woman you want to become?

- Does she have a successful career or business?

- What is my relationship with money?

- Am I afraid to be successful and wealthy?

- What do people tell me that I'm good at the most?

- What do I enjoy doing in my spare time?

- When is the last time I invested in a course to enhance my finances or skill set?

- What were my family's money habits and beliefs?

Her Self-Care

Your self-care is *everything*. I can't express this enough.

Somehow many believe that self-care pertains to hair salons, manicures, pedicures, and massages. It is so much deeper than that, and when done correctly, it can change areas of your life in ways you can't even imagine.

Manicures and pedicures are fabulous, but those things are self-maintenance, not deep self-care. There is a vast difference between the two. Self-maintenance are things you do to maintain your self-care. Something that you probably would do to pamper yourself.

Self-care is something that you do when trying to improve your overall being. It has nothing to do with outward pampering as much as it does with overall health. I'm speaking of mind, body, and soul.

Most of us don't realize that when we think we have a "self-care Saturday," we're having a self-maintenance day.

When was the last time you rested your mind? What about taking a walk to connect with nature and tune in to how you are feeling. When was the last time you've done, girl?

I know, as women, we have a lot on our plate. It's always something for us to do from the children, careers, and relationships.

Therefore, it takes more than a spa day. Your self-care concerns your mental, emotional, spiritual, and soul health. When you address what is consuming you mentally, you will change your emotional state. How we feel is fueled by how we think.

One way I do this is simply by taking a walk. It slows down my thoughts, mind, and emotions. Walking is one of the more underrated forms of emotional release.

Walking has been proven to have mental and physical benefits. This alone is a direct connection to your self-care. You cannot take care of yourself if your mind is not together.

Another tool you can use is journaling. I am not referring to cute and fun journaling, but the journaling that makes you dig into your past and makes you relive moments that you've been trying to forget.

When I wrote my book *Broken But Not Bound*, I talked about my childhood. I thought it would be easy until I began to remember the traumas that I had buried.

The memories flooded in, and I could then identify why my life was in shambles.

As I continued to write, I healed. Going through the emotional pain that comes with change is challenging yet rewarding.

This goes into my next point for successful self-care. Forgiveness. Forgive people who never apologized. Forgive people who you're still waiting for closure from. Let go of the need to understand the reason someone hurt you. Forgive your parents. Forgive yourself.

Forgiveness is another very underrated form of self-care that can free up any mental, spiritual, financial, and emotional blockages. You are less likely to move forward with your life freely without forgiveness. You will lack the ability to reach your full potential.

I hope you noticed that none of what I've shared is geared towards malls and spas. We can hide behind the mask of self-maintenance. Who wants to look beautiful on the outside while wounded on the inside? Not the woman you are becoming! That is what proper self-care is all about.

Your self-care plays a huge factor in your self-love. It's one of the reasons why this chapter is so important. You will never find peace and happiness if you don't love yourself first. And if you're not adequately taking care of yourself, you don't love yourself.

Don't be offended by this. When your self-care only scratches the surface level, you don't care about yourself enough. Everything that you've done in life and every decision you've made either came from loving yourself a lot or not loving yourself enough.

No one cautiously walks around thinking or feeling they don't love themselves, but we don't realize the many ways we do and accept things that make it obvious to other people we don't.

The people we entertain is a clear indicator of our self-esteem and self-love meter. They are tied directly to your self-care. When we love and take care of ourselves properly, we carry a different type of confidence and respect for yourself that everyone around us notices.

Protecting your peace is a form of self-care. You can protect your peace in many ways, but the best way to start is by ending any friendships or relationships that drain you. Remove yourself from groups that cause you to second-guess yourself. Dissociate yourself from family members that bring you anxiety.

Although it can be hard to do, it must be done. Nobody should be pulling from your energy and causing you to be depleted. Nobody. Protecting your peace means protecting your mental health. People driving you crazy is not just a figure of speech; it's a real thing that I'm sure you can relate to.

But you aren't allowing that anymore—no more loyalty to energy vampires and being the nice girl with no boundaries.

Once you've been able to acknowledge these deeper parts of you that need to be cared for, that's when you can spend more time indulging in self-maintenance. The spa days, the brunches, and the endless mimosas. The wine down Wednesdays, bubble bath Fridays, and any other maintenance that goes with your cleansed soul.

Engaging in self-maintenance is like a reward after practicing self-care because self-care isn't always fun. It's deep, emotional, and scary, but it's also very much needed. Nobody has any business perfecting their toes while still having holes in their heart.

But, once you've gotten to where you've been practicing your self-care and heading into more self-maintenance... vacation, vacation, vacation!

I can't express how important it is to take a vacation. Your vacation doesn't have to be expensive; it doesn't have to be in another state, and it doesn't have to be for a certain number of days, but you need to vacation.

Well, the woman I wanted to become lived a laptop lifestyle. She could take her work anywhere in the world and be productive. Although I love how I set up my life, I had to stop working on vacation. It was hard for me to take an actual vacation for a while. I had to learn to take a break and live in the moment.

Work will always be there, but the whole point of a vacation is to get away from work. Embrace and enjoy the scenery of wherever you go. Allow your vacation to rejuvenate you. After returning from a vacation, I am the most creative and at peace version of myself.

I prefer beaches and sand, but if you prefer log cabins, lakes, cottages, snow, or even the excitement of a tourist city, go for it. Do whatever will make you feel like you're on vacation.

Another great thing I love to do is go flower and strawberry picking, and painting pottery. If you're a social media follower of mine, you know that I talk about this often. Doing this brings me so much joy and peace. It's what I call Mindless Feminine Activities. These activities do not require me to think, worry or figure out a solution. It keeps me in my element of being a woman with hobbies and living an exciting life that others view as attractive.

If you haven't tried it before, I recommend doing so.

You can continue doing the spas, waxing, exfoliating, and all that wonderfulness; just be sure to remember which category they fall under. *Self-maintenance.* Although self-maintenance differs from self-care, it's still a required routine.

The same way you wake up every morning and immediately check your phone, you should be saying positive affirmations. In the same way that you make sure your stomach is full, make sure your mind, body, and soul are healthy. This will turn into your new way of life, and you will never want to go back to how you were subconsciously depriving yourself again.

Questions to Ask Yourself

- What type of self–maintenance routine would the woman I'm becoming have?

- Do I feel comfortable going to therapy?

- Do I have a hard time forgiving people?

- Do I confuse self-care with self-maintenance?

- When was the last time I put myself first?

- How well do I keep up with myself?

- When was the last time I took a walk?

- How do I feel about meditating?

- How often do I drink water?

- When was the last time I soaked in a bath?

- Does thinking about my past make me feel uncomfortable?

Her Man

I hope you didn't open this book and rush to this chapter because you would be trying to cheat the process. I know you don't want to do that, right? Good. There is a reason this chapter was so close to the end. Your process is *not* about getting a man. That's the easy part. It's about you, and when you do the work for yourself, high-caliber men will show up.

The man is the byproduct of you becoming a dope woman, and I mean precisely that. Once you become the woman you desire to be for yourself, you can recognize his dopeness. You will *never* have to search and find where the good men are. They'll be drawn to you. You will only have to choose which one is best suited for you.

After you have done what I have suggested in this book, then and only then will you be ready for your man. Again, all the chapters are essential, but I want to highlight your mindset, habits, and femininity when it comes to your man.

When we initially talked about your mindset, we were talking about it from the perspective of it being a benefit to you and you only, but here is how it can play a role in getting to the relationship you want.

Have you ever heard the story of the woman who always cut the butt off the Thanksgiving ham? Her husband would always ask why she did this, and she would tell him that's just the way she does it. She did this for a few more years until, one day, her mom came over for Thanksgiving. Once again, she cut the butt off the ham, and her mom asked, "Why are you doing that?" She said, "Because that's what I saw you do growing up, so that's how I've always done it." Her mom laughed and said, "I only did that because our oven wasn't big enough to fit the entire ham inside. You don't have to cook yours that way; your oven is perfectly fine."

Something as simple as the way you cook can be influenced by what you've seen, and you never thought to question.

In the same fashion, you must recondition your mindset about men. You may be carrying your mother's, grandmother's, aunt's fears, wounds, and beliefs. This includes letting go of old unpleasant experiences with men. You must also remember, the old version of you made those mistakes. Forgive her and move into your new identity.

This means the woman you are becoming will entertain a different caliber of man. You cannot bring your old fears to mingle with the new you. You're either going to let go and get the love you deserve or stay stuck. You can't have both and be successful. It's like trying to drive with your foot on the gas and the break. Yes, it will also take courage, but you have that. You cannot become a new woman and keep the same way of thinking. You will miss out on a great man while subconsciously treating him like the men from your past.

For example, you were dating someone for three months, and you decided to be intimate with him. Afterward, he gradually stopped texting you good morning. He stopped being consistent and stopped planning dates. And just like any woman would be, you feel abandoned, used, and rejected.

Let's also say that before having sex with him, he told you that he wasn't looking for anything serious and just wanted to go with the flow. If a relationship came from it, he would be cool with that too. For starters, this is not the type of guy you should be entertaining in the first place if you're looking for a commitment.

He clarified where he stood and his intentions. Somehow, you thought things were progressing because he was sweet to you, taking you out and making you feel special.

Now let's say that you have transformed into the woman you desire to be and meet another man. This man wants to be married and has shown you he is serious about you. You've dated him for five months, and you finally decided to be intimate with him. He gradually stops texting you good morning, but he still makes time to call and see you.

You would sabotage this by going off on him and telling him that you're more than just sex and that you won't ever let anybody treat you less than you deserve. He would be confused because he doesn't know that he's done wrong.

You only feel this way because it reminds you of your past experience, but you are dealing with two different men. You have to look at the overall context before accusing him of being "just like everybody else." Why didn't you think "*he must be having a long work week?*" Why didn't you tell him that you miss his morning text messages? Why did you assume he was no longer interested in you? Has he ever shown you he wasn't interested in you?

Probably not.

You ultimately used your experience with a man who made it clear he didn't want a relationship with you and compared it to a man expressing and showing you he likes you. Sometimes people get busy. Sometimes people slip. It happens. But you need to know how not to let your old experiences and conditioning affect your love life.

As I said earlier, your mindset and habits are almost the same, so I wanted to paint a picture for you. Did you get it? If so, have you done this before? Because your subconscious mind holds these painful experiences, you may not even realize you are operating in this manner.

Through my experience with men and the seasoned ladies who mentor me, I have learned that they are simple creatures. We make them complex and want them to think as we do. However, from the many years I've worked with women, the bigger issue is, they aren't good enough or deserving of a good man. Or they want strategies on how to snag a man, but that is short lived. It will become exhausting trying to keep up a way of being for a man. What will happen is, he will see that you aren't what you sold him on. Why is this? Because you must become the representative you are pretending to be. Why not? If you know how to be her to attract him, why not do the extra work to transform into her?

The woman you are becoming has a life. She isn't sitting around trying to play hard to get; she is hard to get. The life she created is for her first, and she wants to welcome a wonderful man into it.

One of my male friends told me he was set straight real fast one night by a woman he was dating. He told her he appreciated that she wore lingerie for him every night. She politely told him she was glad he liked it, but it wasn't for him; it was for her.

It was the first time he had ever had a woman tell him that, and it made him even more intrigued with her. I've run across so many women who feel like lingerie is only for a man's pleasure. That couldn't be further from the truth. It is for you to embrace first.

If you are single, these habits may not seem like a big deal, but they are very attractive. Any time I would tell a man I would call him back because it was my pampering time. They would be amazed and respectful of it. They saw how I made myself a priority, and they did the same. You teach people how to treat you by how you treat yourself. If you are married or in a relationship, the same rules apply. Doing this will also aid in tapping more into your feminine side.

It takes 21 days to build a new habit. It is essential to create positive habits now because the man you want is looking for this version of you. Understand that the man you desire is waiting for you on the other side of your switch.

Men crave feminine women because we have something they do not. It's an unexplainable experience. All he knows is how he feels when he is around you. Most of the time, men do not know what they want until they experience it. This is why men like Idris Elba, George Clooney and Adam Levine, who vowed to never get married, are now happily married. Are you a breathtaking experience? It's the energy that he has been deprived of. Why do you think men enjoy the strip club? Hear me out and take notes. Now, some men are there for a sexual reason, and that is to be expected. However, for many, it is the only time they get to experience feminine energy throughout their day because so many women they come across have suppressed it. The funny thing is, they crave this energy so much, they will pay to be around it. At the strip club, women are soft, gentle, kind, pleasant, sensual, soothing, peaceful, flirty, and will stroke the heck out of an ego. Even though they have a motive, pay attention to their method. Your feminine energy is so powerful, and it's up to you to decide how to use it wisely. You have been warned.

I am not telling you to become a stripper, but I am showing you what men crave. The feminine energy also evokes creativity. This is why men can have business meetings in this environment; creative energy surrounds them, amplifying their portfolios.

Your femininity will always be your superpower. Knowing when to lose the battle to win the war is key. Everything doesn't need to be an argument, require your feedback or a discussion. Allowing him to lead and make decisions, even though he will run them by you. *Wink*

Are you feeling uncomfortable again right now? If so, good! The woman you are becoming has no problem operating in this manner because she chose a man whose leadership she could trust. She vetted him properly.

What is vetting, you ask?
Vet
/vet/
verb
Investigate (someone) thoroughly, especially to ensure that they are suitable for a job requiring secrecy, loyalty, or trustworthiness.

You can only vet a man after knowing who you are and what you need. Once you are equipped with this information, you can now get to know him based upon your needs. I asked often, what questions should I ask on a date? I could give you tons of generic questions, but wouldn't it be better to ask questions that are aligned with your core needs?

Once again, the woman you're becoming knows what she needs in a man because she took the time to get to know herself. You will frustrate yourself every time if you don't go through the "getting to know me" process.

Now let's talk about allowing. Do you know how to receive from a man? The woman you're becoming does. She knows what she deserves and welcomes it freely. It's hard to receive as women because we are so used to giving. How often have you received a compliment on what you were wearing, and you said something like, "this old thing, I got this on sale, etc.." instead of saying thank you? This is a sign you do not feel deserving. If you have a hard time receiving a simple compliment, how can you invite a good man into your life? The sabotage is real.

This will require you to make a drastic identity shift, which includes honesty, vulnerability, and the ability to trust yourself. You do not want to choose a man with a lack mentality.

The man you attract after you undergo your mental, emotional, and spiritual transformation will be just what the doctor ordered. When he arrives, you would have done the inner work to receive him without fear.

Now let me warn you that although you are becoming this amazing woman, being in a healthy relationship is going to feel uncomfortable. It could feel too calm. Too right. Too perfect, to the point you dislike him for no reason. This is your subconscious mind... JESSICA once again trying to recreate the toxic relationship patterns that she's familiar with. If there are no red flags, sit there and be loved on. It will feel uncomfortable, but you are changing your wiring.

Whatever you do, do not self-sabotage this. You have cried many nights asking to find someone who would love and cherish you. The work you have done on yourself brought him to you. Enjoy it.

- What type of man would the woman I'm becoming choose?

- What are my core values?

- What was the relationship dynamic between my parents?

- How did the women in my family discuss men?

- Am I ready to be in a healthy relationship? Why or why not?

- What are my three must-haves? No generic answers?

- Why don't I feel good enough? When did this start?

- Do I need to go to therapy?

- Why am I afraid to be vulnerable?

- Why am I afraid of relinquishing control?

- Do I think good men are too good to be true?

- Do I have a hard time finding good men?

- What should I work on before meeting my future husband?

Her Lifestyle

This book provided you with the tools to jumpstart your identity switch. A guide to giving you a visual that you can create whatever life you want when you choose to become a new version of yourself.

As you continue to move forward, you will notice how your reality shifts. You don't see things in your life as they are; you see them as you are. So, the best way to see what you want is to continue your transformation journey. You do not have to wait until December 31st to start your new life; it begins now. You must know exactly what you want, develop habits that support your goals, drop the ones that don't, respond instead of reacting to obstacles and stay the course.

Your lifestyle should consist of the 8 areas below. To make a total life switch, you must address each area.

1 **Career/Business**
2 **Finances and Wealth**
3 **Love Life**
4 **Fun and Entertainment**

This is the fun part. You get to decide! Go big! Your life is the canvas, and you are the artist. Don't limit yourself because you are funneling your life through the eyes and resources of the old you. As you create your new life, I want you to close your eyes and feel what your new life feels like. Where are you? What do you have one? Who is with you? What is the weather like? What do you smell?

You can start by saying one or all the following affirmations:

I am at peace with my mind, body, and soul

I am not struggling financially

I am a money magnet

I always have more than enough

I live an abundant life

Money comes effortlessly

I feel loved, seen and heard

I have successful relationships

Amazing things always happen to me

I am happy and satisfied with my life

108

Saying and believing these things keep you in a believing and receiving state. This leaves no room for doubt or second-guessing. Even if your situation looks like the opposite of what you're saying, you say it anyway because you're speaking as if it's already done, which it will be.

Go as far as changing the meals you cook! Go big! Your life is the canvas and you are the artist.

Be ready to change everything that you've grown accustomed to doing because you've been playing too small!

There is nothing you can't have unless *you* believe you can't have it. We were not put on earth to struggle, be loveless and pay bills. The life you want to live is on the other side of consistency, self-worth and being intentional.

You must know where you want to go in order to choose the best path. I believe in you, and can't wait to see you on the other side, darlin'.

Questions to Ask Yourself

- What type of lifestyle would the woman I'm becoming have?

- Does my current lifestyle represent the life I desire? Why or why not?

- Do I believe I can have a better lifestyle?

- Can I afford to enjoy my life on vacation for two weeks without my bills falling behind?

- Do I have a least 6 months – 1 year of living expenses saved?

- Am I willing to hold myself accountable to achieve my lifestyle goals?

OTHER RESOURCES

www.aprilmason.com

www.aprilondemand.com

Instagram: msaprilmason

Facebook: msaprilmason

TikTok: msaprilmason

DOWNLOAD

All Things Feminine Social Club App inside of your Apple or Google Play Store

Made in the USA
Monee, IL
19 January 2022

89314234R00066